The Irish Potato Famine: The History and Legacy of the Mass Starvation in Ireland During the 19th Century

By Charles River Editors

An illustration depicting the famine

About Charles River Editors

Charles River Editors provides superior editing and original writing services across the digital publishing industry, with the expertise to create digital content for publishers across a vast range of subject matter. In addition to providing original digital content for third party publishers, we also republish civilization's greatest literary works, bringing them to new generations of readers via ebooks.

Sign up here to receive updates about free books as we publish them, and visit Our Kindle Author Page to browse today's free promotions and our most recently published Kindle titles.

Introduction

An illustration depicting Irish emigration

The Irish Potato Famine

""I have called it an artificial famine: that is to say, it was a famine which desolated a rich and fertile island that produced every year abundance and superabundance to sustain all her people and many more. The English, indeed, call the famine a 'dispensation of Providence;' and ascribe it entirely to the blight on potatoes. But potatoes failed in like manner all over Europe; yet there was no famine save in Ireland." – John Mitchel, Young Ireland Movement

Anyone who has ever heard of "the luck of the Irish" knows that it is not something to wish on someone, for few people in the British Isles have ever suffered as the Irish have. As one commissioner looking into the situation in Ireland wrote in February 1845, "It would be impossible adequately to describe the privations which they habitually and silently endure...in many districts their only food is the potato, their only beverage water...their cabins are seldom a protection against the weather...a bed or a blanket is a rare luxury...and nearly in all their pig and a manure heap constitute their only property." Even his fellow commissioners agreed and expressed "our strong sense of the patient endurance which the laboring classes have exhibited under sufferings greater, we believe, than the people of any other country in Europe have to sustain."

Still, in their long history of suffering, nothing was ever so terrible as what the Irish endured during the Great Potato Famine that struck the country in the 1840s and produced massive upheaval for several years. While countless numbers of Irish starved, the famine also compelled many to leave, and all the while, the British were exporting enough food from Ireland on a daily basis to prevent the starvation. Over the course of 10 years, the population of Ireland decreased by about 1.5 million people, and taken together, these facts have led to charges as severe as genocide. At the least, it indicated a British desire to remake Ireland in a new mold. As historian Christine Kinealy noted, "As the Famine progressed, it became apparent that the government was using its information not merely to help it formulate its relief policies, but also as an opportunity to facilitate various long-desired changes within Ireland. These included population control and the consolidation of property through various means, including emigration... Despite the overwhelming evidence of prolonged distress caused by successive years of potato blight, the underlying philosophy of the relief efforts was that they should be kept to a minimalist level; in fact they actually decreased as the Famine progressed."

Although the Famine obviously weakened Ireland and its people, it also stiffened Irish resolve and helped propel independence movements in its wake. By the time the Famine was over, it had changed the face of not just Ireland but also Great Britain, and it had even made its effects felt across the Atlantic in the still young United States of America. *The Irish Potato Famine* looks at the history of the Great Famine and what it produced. Along with pictures and a bibliography, you will learn about the Irish Potato Famine like never before, in no time at all.

The Irish Potato Famine: The History and Legacy of the Mass Starvation in Ireland during the 19th Century

About Charles River Editors

Introduction

   Chapter 1: Accounts of the Destitution

   Chapter 2: No Credence

   Chapter 3: Some Sensible Relief

   Chapter 4: A Sacrifice of Human Life

   Chapter 5: Reports of Misery

   Chapter 6: A Calamity, the Like of Which the World Had Never Seen

   Chapter 7: Sweep Away the Entire Population

   Chapter 8: For the Relief of the Irish Nation

Bibliography

Chapter 1: Accounts of the Destitution

"I regret to say that there is not the slightest mitigation in the accounts of the destitution received today. We are now in the midst of a second winter, the frost and snow of Christmas having apparently reset in with equal if not increased severity, so that any prospect of amelioration is just now as remote as ever." - *The London Times*, February 10, 1846

The first hint that there was a potential problem in the British Isles came in August 1845, when the Prime Minister of Great Britain, Sir Robert Peel, was informed that the "potato blight" that had been a problem in America had made its way to Southern England. While the United States was able to grow enough different crops to offset the potato blight, it was a far greater inconvenience in England. Much worse, he was warned, would be the effect it would have on the people of Ireland, who depended on the potato much like those in Asian countries depended on rice.

Peel

Tragically, the predictions proved correct, and as the blight spread to Ireland the following month, the *Gardener's Chronicle* warned that "the potato murrain has unequivocally declared itself in Ireland. Where will Ireland be in the event of a universal potato rot?" At this time, the British government was offering no answers.

October 1845 brought more bad news, as the poorest among the Irish began digging the potatoes that would have to feed them through the winter. That is when they discovered the true extent of the blight and reached out to the British Parliament for help. To his credit, Peel tried to move quickly to avoid disaster. In 1847, the *Dublin University Magazine* noted, "In the autumn of 1845, it was discovered that a disease had attacked the potato in Ireland, and in several other parts of the world. Of the actual existence of such a disease there was no doubt…Some of the journals in Ireland, supposed most to represent the aristocracy, persisted in vigorously denying the existence of any failure to more than a very partial extent…To profess belief in the existence of a formidable potato blight, was as sure a method of being branded a radical, as to propose to destroy the Church. Sir Robert Peel was then at the head of affairs, and the ministry certainly foresaw the coming calamity. Inquiries were made as to the substance that would be the best and cheapest substitute for the potato. Indian corn was adopted, and without any public excitement on the subject, orders were given by the government for the importation of Indian corn to the amount of L100,000. This timely precaution, and the subsequent judicious distribution of this store, had the effect of bringing the people through the winter of 1845, without exposing them to any sever privations…"

While importing corn solved some of Ireland's problems, it caused a hue and cry among much of the rest of Great Britain because it drove down the price English farmers could expect to get for their grain crops. As a result, Peel was unable to keep the help coming, even though he put his own position on the line. The magazine article continued, "It was, however, the misfortune of famine-stricken Ireland, and a deep misfortune almost all men in Ireland now feel it to be, that party combinations (we say not now, how justifiable or honorable) removed from office the man who had shown himself alone, perhaps, of living statesmen, alive to the exigencies of the crisis, and capable of boldly and efficiently meeting them. It was an occasion upon which no statesman could efficiently serve the country out of office…and with the removal of Peel from office he lost the power of even assisting to obviate the danger, which, we do believe, had he remained in office, he would successfully have met."

While waiting for the corn to arrive, the Irish people began to feel the full brunt of the famine in early 1846. On February 8, the *Cork Reporter* reported, "A large body of the Roman Catholic clergy of the united dioceses of Cloyne and Ross, have originated a movement in favor of the extension of the English Poor Law to this country, so as to insure the right of outdoor relief, not merely to the infirm, the blind, and the half, but to the able bodied laborer driven to the verge of destitution by a chain of circumstances over which, it might be, he could have not control."

One of the most pressing problems was that people continued to hear that they were going to receive more corn, yet they never saw it coming. In the middle of March 1846, the *Cork Reporter* decried the "evils of delay" and wrote that "while parties in the state and elsewhere are squabbling among themselves as to what is to be deemed the starvation test, sickness and famine are already doing their work. The afflicting spectacle of man and wife borne to the grave from fever was witnessed in our streets yesterday. The melancholy procession and the cry by which they were followed, sufficiently attested the class to which they belonged -- they were of the poor. Three of their orphans are struggling with the same malady and remain in the same building from which they were removed. How many, let us ask, must perish before any of the four bills latterly passed is in operation, or any of the food in hand distributed? Are we to have nothing and hear of nothing but precautions? Will the Fabian policy conquer hunger and subdue in pestilence? As yet no family has had a meal of the state-imported corn. It is here -- it is on the way -- it is grinding -- sailing -- travelling from one estuary to another. It is talked of -- one day it is off the harbor, another at the quays; the next it is reloaded and wafted won the river, and the last announcement left it off the coast of Dingle, where the ship that bore it loomed through the mist like the Flying Dutchman, disappearing, perhaps, to attract the anxious gaze of the watchers on some other shore. We have the substantial proof of food being really here in the daily marching and counter-marching of marines and regulars, but beyond that we have no gratification."

A contemporary depiction of an Irish woman and her two kids

Meanwhile, people were so desperate for something to eat that they continued to eat the obviously tainted corn, which naturally spread sickness around the countryside. The *Cork Reporter* article explained, "The people do not well know how to apply or where to come to; the distant parishes have heard rumors, but yet require information. They have received hints and read letters once or twice, but there is no public proclamation of the terms on which they are to apply for sustenance. They have gone on eating or fasting on the tainted potato, imbibing mortal disease, and have sickened, died or starved, while the machinery of grand jury and other intervention was preparing. Food and employment ought to be afforded at once, instantly. We have said so over and over; we repeated the warning until we grew tired of the reiteration. … Unsound potatoes have bred typhus. The sick are in some cases quintupled; contagion is fearful; even the word we fear to write -- cholera is apprehended. Why is this? Where is it to end? Precautions were taken. Every wise and sufficient antidote was contemplated. The plans were faultless, the scheme of the campaign against the double foe of famine and pestilence was without a flaw. Sir R. Peel assures us he had foreseen all that was to happen, but how many are they who have gone to the grave through the wards of the hospitals while he and his colleagues were quarreling and pondering, resigning and resuming office? We repeat our question: what is the number of dead we must first count over before food will begin to be distributed?"

Chapter 2: No Credence

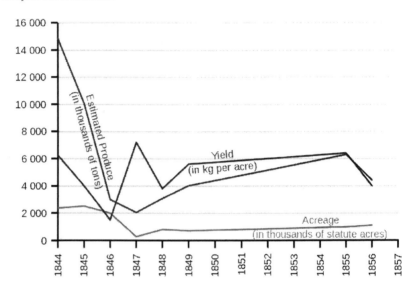

A graph showing the drop in potato production after 1844

"Amid all the talk which we hear about potatoes, we find nothing to guide us to a satisfactory estimate, or even conjecture, as to the actual supply in the country. On one hand we have nothing but fearful forebodings -- the stock is exhausted and famine stares us in the face; on the other, we are told of stores that will bring us safely through the season, and that the noise about scarcity is only a political device. Applied to different districts there may be truth in both. Throughout the controversy we have endeavored to steer clear of extremes. We have given no credence to the exaggerations of even official information, but have endeavored to set before our readers as they came in our way, such accounts as from the opportunities of the writers, appeared most worthy of attention. We believe the fact to be that in some places there is a sufficiency -- in others, the reverse; and we are not without hope that with the precautions taken by Government, we shall be able to struggle on until the new crop comes in." - Letter to the Editor of the *Dublin Times*

Even when the corn arrived, there continued to be problems because it was not yet ground up and there were few mills in Ireland suitable for grinding corn. When the corn was grounded up and distributed, it still had to be cooked carefully and for a long time or it would cause serious digestive problems. In fact, the same might also be said for the legislation surrounding the corn's use. The Irish political leader John Mitchel was fighting hard to keep the corn coming into Ireland, complaining publicly on February 14 about "the wretched way in which the famine was being trifled with" in spite of "millions of human beings in Ireland having nothing to eat." He later added that while his fellow members could not seem to agree on what they ought to do about hunger among the Irish, "they agree most cordially in the policy of taxing, prosecuting and ruining them."

Mitchel

Pleas for help continued to pour in, as A.F. Rocher, the Mayor of Cork, wrote to Lord Heytesbury, the Lieutenant Governor and General Governor of Ireland, on March 11, 1846: "My Lord -- I take the liberty of addressing your Excellency in compliance with a resolution adopted by the trustees of the Poor Relief Fund of this city, and as the chairman of the meeting held on Friday last. It is unnecessary for me to go into the numerous and most painful details of the deep distress of the poor of Cork, and of its alarming progress; but I am directed lay before your excellency the humble prayers of the committee, that immediate measures may be taken for a general issue and sale of Indian corn and oatmeal to the poorer classes, who are at this moment for the most part subsisting on rotten potatoes, and among whom disease is already making fearful ravages."

While the politicians haggled about who was going to do what for whom, journalists continued to warn about the dangers facing Irish farmers, most of whom had lost as much as half their food supply. Peel's primary opponent, Lord Russell, was a firm believer in laissez-faire economics, and he was even quoted as claiming "the judgement of God sent the calamity to teach the Irish a lesson." Many agreed with him, including James Wilson, who wrote in *The Economist*, "It is no man's business to provide for another. … If left to the natural law of distribution, those who deserve more would obtain it." However, with the law of supply and demand governing potato sales, the poor were slowly being winnowed out. The *Cork Reporter* noted in early March 1846, "But on the part of the poor, the struggle will be severe. Even at present, the price is beyond their reach; but this is in a great measure owing to the habit of forestalling. The potatoes are purchased before they enter the market, and there retailed to the consumer at an enormous profit. Thus while they bring in the market from 9d to 11d per weight, they are selling from the boats at 7 d. . . . During the week a gentleman, observing four cartloads of fine-looking potatoes in the street, asked the owner the price. The answer was, 'Sir, we couldn't sell them under sixpence;' yet though offered at those terms, they had been brought from within a mile of Mallow. The consumer, however, was probably nothing better for the moderation of the owner, for we dare say they fell into the hands of the forestaller, and were by him sold at nearly double the sixpence. We mention these facts, as it is well that, while we take all prudent precautions to meet any danger of which there may be reasonable apprehension, people should be warned against lending themselves to either pecuniary or political designs by exciting fears and spreading alarms for which there is no foundation."

Russell

While half the potato crop had been decimated, the blight did not strike all farmers equally, but even for those who had at least a few potatoes to sell to those desperately in need, they had no way of getting them to their potential customers. Meanwhile, people continued to have a problem adjusting to eating another foreign substance: cornbread. Hunger began to lead to civil unrest, with the *Limerick Reporter* in Dublin writing in late March, "'Apprehension' of all kinds (of fever and famine inclusive) seem to be the order of the day in Ireland. The intelligence from Limerick this morning prognosticates an early outbreak in the 'city of the violated treaty,' induced partly (and not unnaturally) by the rapid decrease of the people's food, and partly by the repugnance of the paupers of the workhouse to the 'partial' use of Indian meal as an article of diet. This is really, and in all conscience, 'too bad.' Bread made of this flour has been for some days on sale in the metropolis, and from its wholesome and nutritious qualities, as well as its cheapness, meets with a rapid consumption among all classes, proving a most fortunate speculation for such bakers as have laid in large stocks of this species of grain. The Limerick Reporter of yesterday thus alludes to the anticipated disturbances and actual revolt of the inmates of the poorhouses."

Of course, it did not help that even the cornmeal had to be rationed and paid for, often by people with no income and little else in the way of food. Farming was never a cash venture during the 19th century, and especially not in Ireland, where families grew potatoes and whatever else they could during the summer and lived on it during the winter. A surplus of anything could be sold for a little extra cash, but the blight wiped out both the food and the potential money, creating a dire situation. The *Limerick* continued, "For the last few days symptoms of an outbreak for food have manifested themselves in this city; and we believe it was actually arranged that it should have taken place yesterday. To anticipate the brewing mischief the Commissary General ordered the Indian meal to be sold to the people; and yesterday, at the Exchange, it was retailed at 1 pence per pound, under the superintendence of the police. Not more than two pounds of it would be sold to any person at a time. Some of the poor seemed most anxious to get it, while others said it was 'nothing better than sawdust.' We understand that many are dissatisfied that it was not distributed gratuitously; while some say this would be no great compliment, for that it is hardly worth giving away. They say, too, that if it were not for the menaced emote not a grain of the meal would be sold for the next two months, and that it would have the effect of preventing them from carrying their plans into execution."

Concerned as always about an actual revolution being fomented, the British government cracked down hard on the suffering people, who at the same time often seemed to want to cause trouble. According to the *Limerick*, "Among the precautions that have been taken to meet any infraction of the public peace, special constables have been sworn in, and there can be manner of doubt that every available force will be brought operation against lawless violence. It was with unfeigned regret we learned yesterday that workhouse paupers -- men, women and children -- turned out in the morning (when it was presented to them for the first time for breakfast) against the uses of stir about, consisting of half oatmeal and half Indian corn. A ton of the latter had been purchased...in order to try it. It was mixed with half oatmeal, and made into hasty pudding, and when it was served up nearly all the women, most of the children and every man, save seven, refused to eat it. That this was the result of a conspiracy there can be no doubt, for the majority of those who refused to eat it did not taste it to try whether they would like it or not; but having made up their minds beforehand, they determined to fast rather than eat it. We think the master and the guardians will be sadly wanting in their duty if they do permit them to adopt their own alternative, until they are brought to these senses, except such as the medical gentleman will say it does not agree with."

Chapter 3: Some Sensible Relief

"The winter of 1846-7, and the succeeding spring, were employed in a series of utterly unavailing attempts to use the 'Labor Rate Act,' so as to afford some sensible relief to the famishing people. Sessions were held, as provided by the Act, and the landed proprietors liberally imposed rates to repay such government advances as they thought needful; but the unintelligible directions constantly interrupted them, and, in the meantime, the peasantry, in the wild, blind hope of public relief, were abandoning their farms and letting the land lie idle." - John Mitchel, 1876

In March, Sir Peel was able to get the Labor Rate Act to Ireland passed through the British Parliament, authorizing Irish officials to tax local districts and thus raise money to hire needy people to do public works. The Act granted further money as aid to those areas that were so destitute that no money could be raised. As one man writing in April 1847 explained, "The provisions of the Labor Rate Act were simple enough. In every barony which the Lord Lieutenant proclaimed in a state of distress, extraordinary presentment sessions were to be held, at which the magistrates and cess-payers were to have the power of presenting for public works to an indefinite extent, subject only to the control of the Board of Works. The sums so presented were to be at once advanced by the Treasury, to be replaced by instalments that would spread the repayment of the entire, with interest, over a period varying at the discretion of the Treasury, from four to twenty years…In addition to the enormous expenditure under the Labor Rate Act, it must be remembered that, in many districts, the landed proprietors undertook to employ all the poor independently of any such provision; that, in others, the provisions of the summary Drainage Act were made available for the same purpose, and that sums that never or can be calculated distributed as gratuitous relief -- sums ostensibly given which appeared in no list of charity subscriptions, which yet form by far the largest proportion of what has been so given; and remembering all this, some estimate may be formed of what has been done by the holders of property in Ireland for the suffering poor…"

Unfortunately, while the plan sounded good on paper, it contained several serious flaws. The first was that the work given was forbidden by law from being profitable. For example, this meant the laborers could not build railroads because there were no new ones authorized to run in Ireland, and they could not seed meadows because that might give the Irish husbandman an advantage over his English counterpart. Thus, the hired workers could only build roads and bridges that were neither needed nor wanted. The writer addressed this when he wrote, "We believe and trust that the demoralizing effect of this upon the habits of the Irish laborer have been overrated; partly, perhaps, because the Irish laborer had few lessons or habits of patient industry to unlearn. What we regret is, the lost opportunity of inculcating better habits. Had these laborers been taught to feel that they were employed upon that which it was of real importance should be done-- had they been employed, under active discipline and careful superintendence, in the formation of the earthwork of railway, or engaged in the reclamation of some waste land, how well might they have been taught the lesson, that the remuneration of labor must, in the long run, depend, in a great degree, upon its productiveness. The employment given under the Labor Rate Act had a double fault; the wages were too low, and the work too light; it taught the people neither side of the lesson which employers and laborers in Ireland equally need to learn – 'a good day's wages for a good day's work.'"

Another flaw was that the people hired were too weak to do manual labor. The author castigated the Parliament for creating this situation: "It is difficult to trace this history without indignation. We can understand the verdict of the coroner's jury, who in days, when inquest were held in Ireland upon the bodies of the men found dead upon the highway, returned upon the body of a man who died in starvation while toiling at the public works, and fell dead of exhaustion with the implements of labor in his hand, a verdict of murder against the ministers who had neglected the first responsibility of government. Can we wonder if the Irish people believe -- and believe it they do -- that the lives of those who have perished, and who will perish, have been sacrificed by a deliberate compact to the gains of English merchants, and if this belief has created among all classes a feeling of deep dissatisfaction, not only with the ministry but with English rule..."

The final and most damning flaw was that the Act contained a clause saying that the government would in no way intervene in the food supply. The author of the 1847 article saved his most virulent criticism for that: "The introduction of the Labor Rate Act was coupled by a declaration on the part of the premier, which appeared almost to amount to a pledge, that with the supply of food to the country government did not intend to interfere; that this should be left entirely to the ordinary resources of commercial enterprise; and that government were resolved in no manner to interfere with the ordinary operations of the speculators or traffickers in human food...Tell us not that it was beyond the power of the combinations, which the strength of the British Empire could have wielded, to have brought to the ports of Ireland subsistence for all her people...The opportunity was lost; and Britain is now branded as the only civilized nation which would permit her subjects to perish of famine, without making a national effort to supply them with food..."

In words that look like they could have come from a more modern debate over the American welfare system, the author complained, "We do not undervalue the activity, the omnipresence of commercial enterprise, compared with the partial and cumbrous effects that the best directed commissariat could make. Government might however have fulfilled this duty without throwing over the aid of this enterprise; its contract with merchants for two or three million of quarters of wheat and Indian corn, might have still left all of commercial activity and enterprise in the service of the supply. We confess, compared with the magnitude of the occasion, we see no reason why government might not have contracted for a supply of Indian corn sufficient to prevent any man in Ireland from starving. The offer of such a contract would have stimulated, not retarded, commercial enterprise. It would have bid the corn of the world to our shores; it would have made the poor Irish peasant a sharer in the supremacy of the British Empire, and saved this country from the horrors with which it is now inflicted..."

On June 29, 1846, Sir Robert Peel resigned as prime minister, discouraged by his inability to get legislation passed and having lost the support of his constituency. Lord Russell took his place and immediately put an end to the programs Peel had established on behalf of the Irish people. To compensate, some grain continued to come into the country, charitable organizations such as the Society of friends continued to raise money to help, and farmers planted more potatoes, praying that that year's crop would be a good one. However, as Fall again rolled around, it was obvious that the blight had only spread further into the countryside. The government did step in again to help, but it would soon prove to be too little and too late for many people. The entire 1846 crop was completely wiped out, and by December, nearly 350,000 people were working in public works jobs, which provided too little income to meet their needs. *The Wexford Independent* reported in mid-December, "Our accounts from the northern parts of this country are most deplorable. What the poor people earn on the public works is barely sufficient to support them. All their earnings go for food; and the consequence is, that they have nothing left to procure clothing. Since the extreme cold set in, sickness and death have accordingly followed in its train. Inflammation of the lungs, fevers, and other maladies, resulting from excessive privation, have been bearing away their victims. Many have died in the course of last week; and the illness in every case was traceable to the want of clothing and firing, if not of sufficient food."

Chapter 4: A Sacrifice of Human Life

"The new year opened gloomily in Ireland. By this time the appalling extent of the calamity, and the inefficiency of the measures adopted to meet it, were, at least, partially understood. A vague sense of alarm possessed men's minds. The terror was, perhaps, exaggerated, because the evils apprehended were indefinite. The public eye was shocked by whole columns of the daily newspapers occupied exclusively with deaths by starvation. Men's hearts failed them with fear, for looking for the things which should come. The landlords saw ruin in the enormous imports which the Labor Rate Act placed upon their estates -- the merchant and the trader feared it in the general stagnation which they anticipated as the consequence of general distress. Rents were in many parts of the country withheld, and alarmists stated were so universally. It is impossible to conceive a more gloomy picture than that presented by Irish society at the close of the disastrous year of '46…" - The *Dublin University Magazine*

On January 8, 1847, the *Cork Reporter* published a story from Bantry which began, "It is my painful duty to inform you of six inquests held here this day, before Mr. Samuel Hutchins and Mr. Richard White, magistrates for the county. The jury unanimously agreed without a moment's hesitation, that the following persons came to their deaths by starvation." From there, it continued to list the sad stories of six people who had died, naming them in most tragic terms:

- "Catherine Sheehan, a child, two years old, who died on the 26th of December last, and had lived for several days previous to her death on sea weed, part of which was produced by Dr. McCarthy, who held a post mortem examination on her body. The other details in this case are most heart-rending.
- Michael Sullivan died at Skahana, on or about the 4th of December, from the effects of eating too hearty a meal, which he had received through charity, after being previously exhausted from overlong fasting.
- Richard Finn was conveyed into this town on the 14th of December, in a car, for the purpose of taking him to the workhouse, when in the street, the Very

Rev. Thomas Barry, parish priest, was obliged to hear confession before the public, and before he had time to complete his sacred duties the poor man expired.

- John Driscoll was working on one of the public works on the 29th of December; on his return home he fell exhausted for want of food, and was found dead in the mountain of Glounlough on the following morning. His wife proved that he had eaten nothing for two days previous to his death, except a small quantity of boiled wheat, and that he frequently had a similar fast.
- Jeremiah Carthy entered the shop of Mr. Robert Vickery, of this town, when he fell senseless, and died in three hours after at the workhouse, though being kindly attended to by the Rev. Mr. Freeman. Dr. Jagoe, and the family, before his removal.
- Michael Linehan was found dead on the lands of Ibane on the 18th of December last. He was on his way home from Bantry after purchasing some food for his mother and brother (which were all his family) who were then lying in fever; there were some turnip peels or skins found in his stomach."

Other papers continued to mourn the deaths of many of their readers, including the *Cork Reporter*, which on January 10 published an article by Jeremiah O'Callaghan about the dire situation in Ballydehob in County Cork. The article asserted, "Since my last report, deaths are fearfully on the increase in this locality. Four have died in the immediate vicinity of this village within the last few days. In the mountain districts they die unknown, unpitied and in most instances unburied for weeks. Yesterday a man was discovered half concealed in a pigsty, in such a revolting condition that humanity would shrink at a description of the body. It was rapidly decomposing; but no neighbor has yet offered his services to cover the loathsome remains. Death has taken forcible possession of every cabin. ...I have just learned that in the neighborhood of Crookhaven they are buried within the walls of their huts. They have in most cases forgotten the usual ceremony of interment. The living are so consumed by famine they are unable to remove the dead. The Examiner could scarcely contain the names of all who have perished for the last month."

Other stories were published from Bantry, also in County Cork, where "[i]n the parish of Kilmore 14 died on Sunday; 3 of these were buried in coffins, 11 were buried without other covering than the rags they wore when alive. And one gentleman, a good and charitable man, speaking of this case, says 'The distress is so appalling, that we must throw away all feelings of delicacy;' and another says, 'I would rather give 1 shilling to a starving man than 4 shillings 6 pence for a coffin.'"

Comments like this were published throughout the paper that day, including stories like these:

- "140 died in the Skibbereen Workhouse in one way; 3 have died in one day! And Mr. M'Carthy Downing states that 'they came into the house merely and solely for the purpose of getting a coffin.'
- "The Rev. Mr. Clancy visits a farm, and there, in one house, 'he administered the last rites of religion to six persons.' On a subsequent occasion, he 'prepared for death a father and daughter lying in the same bed.'
- "The Rev. Mr. Caulfield sees '13 members of one family lying down in fever.'
- "The Rev. Mr. Fitzpatrick retires to rest at 3 o'clock in the morning, and rise after a couple hours' heavy sleep. It is the same with his co-adjudicators.
- Dr. Donovan solemnly assures a public meeting that the people are 'dropping in dozens about them.'"

A few weeks later, the *Mayo Constitution* reported, "In the neighborhood of Newport, on Sunday morning last, a poor man, named Mulloy, was found on the road side. His emaciated frame betokened that his death was the result of want. He was a native of Burrishcole. On Friday last a poor man died at Deradda, near Newport, of actual hunger, leaving a family to follow in rapid succession. On Saturday, a poor man was also found expiring from exhaustion at Rooskeen, and notwithstanding relief being brought, the poor man died, food having come too late! ... In this village there is not a family that do not appear likely to fall victim to famine. ... On the same day on the body of William Sheridan, at Cloondes. The deceased had been in a great state of destitution, and going from one village to another he fell into a small rivulet which he attempted to cross, and from his debility was unable to extricate himself! Verdict – 'Death by drowning, but attributed to starvation.'"

Ultimately, one of the reports summed up the frightening state of affairs at this point: "That we feel it is our duty to state, under the correction of the Court, that it is our opinion that if the Government of the country shall persevere in its determination of refusing to use the means available to it for the purpose of lowering the price of food, so as to place it within the reach of the laboring poor, the result will be a sacrifice of human life from starvation to a frightful extent, and endangerment of property and of the public peace.*"*

By February 1847, even *The London News* was carrying stories of the tragedy, with artist James Mahoney writing, "We first proceeded to Bridgetown, a portion of which is shown in the right hand distance of the sketch; and there I saw the dying, the living, and the dead, lying indiscriminately upon the same floor, without anything between them and the cold earth, save a few miserable rags upon them. To point to any particular house as a proof of this would be a waste of time, as all were in the same state; and, not a single house out of 500 could boast of being free from death and fever, though several could be pointed out with the dead lying close to the living for the space of three or four, even six days, without any effort being made to remove the bodies to a last resting place."

Chapter 5: Reports of Misery

"I...saw little until we came to Clonakilty, where the coach stopped for breakfast; and here, for the first time, the horrors of the poverty became visible, in the vast number of famished poor, who flocked around the coach to beg alms: amongst them was a woman carrying in her arms the corpse of a fine child, and making the most distressing appeal to the passengers for aid to enable her to purchase a coffin and bury her dear little baby. This horrible spectacle induced me to make some inquiry about her, when I learned from the people of the hotel that each day brings dozens of such applicants into the town. After leaving Clonakilty, each step that we took westward brought fresh evidence of the truth of the reports of the misery, as we either met a funeral or a coffin at every hundred yards, until we approached the country of the Shepperton Lakes. Here, the distress became more striking, from the decrease of numbers at the funerals, none having more than eight or ten attendants, and many only two or three." – James Mahoney, "Sketches From Western Ireland," published in *The London News* in February 1847

As the disaster continued with no end in sight, there were vocal protests aimed at the absentee landlords who lived in comfort in England while renting out their farms piecemeal in Ireland. The newspaper reported, "Mr. M'Carthy Downing proclaims a fact damning the character of the Skibbereen landlords. For two months past the secretary of the Relief Committee has been importuning the landlords of the district; and with what result, think you, reader? Out of four parishes, comprising the relief district, but nine subscriptions have been received, after two months' begging." Still, out of fairness, it was reported that many of the local landlords seemed to be interested in the welfare of the less fortunate: "Mr. Downing excepts these landlords who reside in the town, whose contributions have been generous -- even excessive. ... Lord Midleton's agent (Mr. Foley) assembled his Lordship's tenants a day or two ago, and allowed them on behalf of his Lordship, from 25 to 75 per cent in their rents! the poorer tenants paying but one-fourth of the whole rent; and so on, up to the comfortable farmers, who have large holdings, and who have been allowed one-fourth for their losses. And not only has his Lordship done so much, but he will do more -- immediately recommence the quay at Cove, which will afford large employment to tradesmen and laborers, and at a rate of wages that will allow them to live. As a commentary on certain facts stated by Mr. Downing of a noble proprietor of this country, who holds land in Skibbereen -- Lord Banden -- we may mention that last year -- when the distress was only partial, and there were no coffinless dead -- Lord Midleton subscribed to all the committees on his estates. We heartily cry, God bless Lord Midleton!"

At the same time, the *Carlow Sentinel* was reporting similar deaths and calling upon the absentee landowners to intervene. In an article called "Progress of Distress," one author wrote, "With feelings of deep regret for the welfare of the extensive district of Ballickmoylter, comprising the large barony of Slievemarigue, we learn that all hopes have vanished of actual provision for the wants of the population, unless the Government come forward and that speedily, with liberal measures of relief. In these times for they are times of peril -- men must speak out; and we shall do our duty fearlessly in calling on the non-residential proprietors to come forward and to lend their cooperation or they will, when too late, regret the consequences of their neglect. In the Ballickmoyler district, Queen's County, a few have, it is true, contributed; but where are the names of the Earl Kenmore, or of the Earl of Portarlington, upon whose estates a vast mass of hideous poverty exists? We have not heard that 1 shilling of their money has yet been contributed, although their agents draw large sums from the extensive estates of these two noblemen in the awfully distressed district to which we refer. We have heard, but cannot say the rumor is true, that Sir Charles Coote, M.P., has only forwarded the relief fund the paltry sum of 10 pounds. Can this be true? We really cannot credit the assertion that a wealthy baronet, of large estate in a barony of the country which he represents, with a vast means of pauperism in the district, and a great number of starving people on his estate, would only contribute a sum of 10 pounds! If he has been so fortunate as to send 1 shilling more we shall apologize for our error in the cause of humanity and the poor of our country."

As more people died, more became desperate. As if the hunger wasn't bad enough, people had to watch neighbors dropping dead and wondering who would be next, including possibly themselves or a family member. Naturally, people continued to rail against the increasing prices and scarcity of grain. The *Cork Reporter* reported in an article entitled "Further Rise in the Prices of Grain," "Notwithstanding the unprecedented arrivals of grain into the port of Dublin, prices still continue to advance. At the Corn Exchange today considerable excitement prevailed and wheat, according to official market note, went up 1 shilling 6 pence...As before remarked, the supplies are pouring in from all quarters; the river is filled with shipping, containing cargoes of flour and other breadstuffs, and the greatest inconvenience is felt from the want of sufficient storage to remedy which temporary sheds have been erected along the north wall at the Custom-house; but even with this makeshift the accommodation is extremely defective. It is the opinion of some of the leading factors here that there will be no material (if any) reduction in the price of bread for two months to come; but that about the middle of March the foreign arrivals must tell, and that speculators may as well be prepared in time for a tremendous reaction."

People who might not have rose up to fight for food for themselves began to threaten violence in order to get enough food to keep their families alive. For instance, according to the *Reporter*, in Dublin in January, "Before 8 o'clock this morning a mob consisting of between 40 and 50 persons, many of them boys, commenced an attack upon the bakers' shops in the neighborhood of summer hill, Britain Street and Abbey Street. Owing to the early hour and the unexpectedness of the outbreak, they were enabled to carry on their depredations without let or hindrance. The rioters had the appearance of country people, and came from the northern outlets of the city. When they had reached Abbey Street two policemen interfered, and endeavored to disperse the crowd, but without any effect, several men exclaiming that they had been without food for 24 hours, and that bread they should have."

As the winter wore on, conditions worsened, and one writer reported, "Poor Coughlan, of the

Board of Works, was crawling home a few nights ago, when hunger and exhaustion seized him within a few yards of his house, where was found the following morning.... If the present system of road making be obstinately persevered in, West Carberry may be properly designated a universal grave-yard." Another article told several similar stories: "On the same day, on the body of James Brislane, at Kilrimmin. The deceased was put on the public works a few days previous to his death, and was hastening on Saturday evening to the office of the pay-clerk, but being very weak from want of food, he fell on the way, and was found dead next morning. Verdict -- 'death by starvation.' On Monday, the 8th, on the body of Pat Howley, at Smisfield. The deceased was employed on the public works, and was found lying on the road, where he had fallen, by a person passing by; when removed to the nearest habitation he died shortly after. Verdict -- 'Death by starvation.'"

With so many people now too weak to work, the public works projects were replaced by workhouses, where people could work indoors, and soup kitchens, which distributed food to those too weak to work. The *Cork Reporter* published the following resolutions passed in Dublin in early January 1846:

> "Resolved: That the workhouse being now fully occupied, there being no fewer than 499 inmates (the house being calculated for only 400), and great destitution prevailing in many parts of the union, the master be instructed, in any case in which a destitute person may present himself with a guardian's order for provisional admission, before sending such person away to give him a meal, consisting of a dinner's ration to be eaten in the house, and to charge same against the union at large.

> "Resolved: That it is also expedient that a room should be procured in the differing districts within the union where destitution prevails; that such room be declared a poorhouse...for the purpose of affording additional relief under the present very extraordinary circumstances of the country. That the guardians make a list of the destitute in those districts, that that after due inquiry, provisional order be given entitling such persons a meal to be eaten in the room so declared a poor house, within each district. The meal to consist of a pint of soup or mill, and 1 1/2 lb. of brown bread for adults, and for children in proportion. That it be fully understood that this mode of relief is only intended to meet the present distressing emergency and that it shall cease with the emergency, or when there is accommodation in the house."

Chapter 6: A Calamity, the Like of Which the World Had Never Seen

"Ireland is now, in one sense, in the midst, in another sense, we fear, in the beginning of a calamity, the like of which the world has never seen. Four millions of people, the majority of whom were always upon the verge of utter destitution, have been suddenly deprived of the sole article of their ordinary food. Without any of the ordinary Channels of commercial intercourse, by which such a loss could be supplied, the country has had no means of replacing the withdrawal of this perished subsistence, and the consequence has been, that in a country that is called civilized, under the protection of the mightiest monarchy upon earth, and almost within a day's communication of the capital of the greatest and richest empire in the world, thousands of our fellow-creatures are each day dying of starvation; and the wasted corpses of many left unburied in their miserable hove]s, to be devoured by the hungry swine; or to escape this profanation, only to diffuse among the living the malaria of pestilence and death." - *The Dublin University Magazine*

The second blight on the potatoes created a downward spiral of crop failure and hunger because, unlike most vegetables, potatoes are not grown from seeds but from other healthy potatoes that are stored away through the winter to be planted the following spring. Thus, the blight didn't just kill the crop it attacked but also damaged future crops, especially since the "seed potatoes" might still carry the contagion. Making matters worse, many farmers who were desperate for something to eat exacerbated things by trying to plant the potatoes too early in the season. The *Derry Journal* reported on this on February 6, 1847: "In consequence of the failure of the potato crop, for the last two seasons, farmers appear inclined to plant earlier; and we have already observed what may be considered, for this season, extensive preparations for proceeding with that operation. In some localities, such as Inch, and the parish of Ardstraw, a sufficiency of seed may be calculated on; but in most districts the want of the requisite amount of seed, and also the deficiency of manure, on the part of the cottiers, who to help themselves through the present distress, have disposed of their manure heaps, and who have hitherto been the greatest producers of this crop, induce us to believe that not more than half of the crop planted last year will be put down this season..."

On top of that, other crops were also suffering during this period, including the all-important wheat: "The wheat crop at one time showed signs of recovering that unhealthfulness which we noticed in our last report; but we regret to say that latterly it has retrograded in most fields, which the excessive rains only can account for. The plants are generally thin on the ground, and their appearance anything but vigorous; but a good spring may yet bring this crop into a promising condition. Owing to the favorable weather at the commencement of the month, a considerable breadth of ground was put down with spring sown wheat; and we should think that by this time there is a full average of that grain committed to the soil."

While there was still hope that the wheat and potatoes might make a future crop, there were many who would not live to see it without help. The *Belfast Chronicle* observed, "The import of breadstuffs and provisions generally into Belfast has been on a very extensive scale during the last ten days. Almost every steamer which arrives from Liverpool, Glasgow or Adrossen brings, as the most important portion of her cargo, Indian corn and meal, peas and flour...Donegal quay was literally a curiosity on Monday -- from the water's edge all across to the stores it was densely covered with bags of Indian corn, sacks of peas, and barrels of flour, and the passenger could with difficulty make his way through the narrow passes and labyrinthine windings of this accumulation of good things. In addition to these arrivals coastwise, immense quantities are being daily landed from foreign ports, the latest of these being the Chusan, from New Orleans, with nearly 9000 bushels of Indian corn, arrived here on Monday and a number of other vessels from Philadelphia, Nantes, Venice, St. Michael's, & c. More are expected, and as a considerable reaction has already taken place in the markets, we think it highly improbably that prices of grain will tend yet lower."

In spite of the extensive imports, there was still not enough food to go around, and people continued to die, with dozens starving to death everyday throughout Ireland. On March 1, 1847, an Irishman, Father Newel, wrote from Oranmore, "The wholesale destruction of human life, occurring here from want of the necessities of life, is fast approximating to what we have read and heard of Skibbereen a few weeks ago, and we shuddered to have to record deaths from starvation by 'units,' but now, alas, we have to compute them by dozens! No less than 54 individuals (men, women, children) have perished of want since December last in the parishes of Oranmore and Ballinacourty; and if the Government, from any compunctious feelings, shall require to ascertain, through their 'Relief Commissioners,' the number of starved wretches provided for in the grave, I shall be able to furnish them with a truly black list, well authenticated, showing the names, and residences of the person victimized here, to the so much spoken of political economy of our rulers."

As the dead piled up literally and figuratively around the community, it became obvious that some of the niceties of burial would have to be dispensed with. Father Newel lamented, "Hitherto, the Religion Committee here have given coffins for the interment of starved dead -- but they are becoming so numerous now that it has been resolved, instead of procuring the common decency of burial for the dead, to reserve the relief fund for the support of the living. I fear much that the want of coffins for the burial of the dead will cause them to be unburied, and to generate infection, more disastrous to human life than the want of food itself. The unusual occurrence here of a human being having been interred without the decency of a coffin took place (as I have heard) in the parish of Ballinacourty a few days ago, when the corpse, after five or six days unburied, was at last sacked up in a coarse canvas and deposited in its parent earth. Another horrifying circumstance occurred near Oranmore, of a poor wretched woman named Redington, perishing during the night time, and in the morning her lifeless body was found partially devoured by rats."

Newel's veiled reference to the "Relief Commissioners" sent by the government to help only served to make public what many others were saying: the government, under Lord Russell, was not doing enough to help stop the suffering and to save the lives of its people. As one letter to the editor of the Galway Mercury complained, "The distress in Loughrea at present is at its utmost height; and any alleviation of that daily increasing distress need not be expected, at least from the Whig Government. That such is the general and growing opinion of almost the entire rural population might be easily inferred from the expressions of unqualified condemnation which were given vent to by all of them with whom I, on this day, happened to hold any conversation. They believe that the Government are determined to systematically put to death one half of the people. With such an opinion daily gaining ground, it is not easy to calculate how long, or why, the Whigs ought to remain in place and power. Under their regime provisions have risen to double the famine price. On this day (Thursday) wheat has been sold at from 55 shillings to 60 shillings per barrel, and oats reached up to the enormous price of from 29 shillings to 30 shillings per barrel, and who can tell but that, a few markets hence, the above articles may reach so high as to be almost above purchase. It is no wonder then that the people should be panic-stricken, especially when the wisest and best amongst us has no hope in the Whig Administration."

Chapter 7: Sweep Away the Entire Population

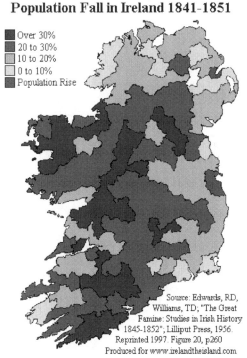

Population Fall in Ireland 1841-1851

- Over 30%
- 20 to 30%
- 10 to 20%
- 0 to 10%
- Population Rise

Source: Edwards, RD, Williams, TD; "The Great Famine: Studies in Irish History 1845-1852"; Lilliput Press, 1956. Reprinted 1997. Figure 20, p260 Produced for www.irelandtheisland.com

Unlike the rest of this site, this map is declared to be in the public domain.

A map detailing the population drop in Ireland during the decade of the Famine

"'Death by starvation' has ceased to be an article of news, and day by day multitudes of our population are swept down into the pit -- literally the pit -- in which the victims of the famine are interred. ... Nearly a month ago the deaths that had resulted in one shape or another from starvation were estimated at 240,000. ... In one...division of the county Cork...out of a population of 16,000, the deaths in the early part of March were averaging 70 a day, a rate of mortality that would sweep away the entire population in about eight months..." - *The Dublin University Magazine*

On February 20, 1847, Parliament passed the "Temporary Relief of Destitute Persons in Ireland," also known as the Poor Law Act. According to a writer at Dublin University, the bill was important in that it admitted for the first time that the government was dealing with a permanent, not temporary, crisis. According to the author, "Relief Commissioners or Finance Committees, appointed by the Lord Lieutenant, are given by this act an unlimited power of taxing the landed interests of Ireland, a power that may indeed be exercised of all landed property in Ireland. In every electoral division, under the Poor-Law in which the Lord Lieutenant considers it expedient that the act should be put in force, a Relief Committee is to be formed.... This committee is to make out lists of all persons within their districts entitled to be relieved, and the estimate of the expense...upon which the Lord Lieutenant issues his warrant to the poor-law guardians to assess upon tenements liable to the poor-rate that sum, and all the expense of the staff necessary for the execution of the act, either upon the union at large, or the electoral division, as he shall judge expedient; the entire amount of such expenditure, unlike that of the Labor Rate Act, must be levied by an immediate rate. The treasury is indeed authorized to advance a sum of 300,000 pounds in anticipation of those rates, but this is plainly a mere temporary accommodation, pending the collection of the rate."

The main problem with this plan was that the landowners were taxed to meet the needs of those living on their holdings. Therefore, it was often expedient to kick the needy off the land they were renting rather than pay the tax. While records were not kept of these evictions during the first years under which the law was in force, between 1849 and 1854, more than 250,000 were removed from the land many had farmed for generations. This situation obviously exacerbated the problem of poverty and starvation rather than address it. Doctor D. Donovan later wrote of one such family, "On my return home, I remembered that I had yet a visit to pay; having in the morning received a ticket to see six members of one family, named Barrett, who had been turned out of the cabin in which they lodged, in the neighborhood of Old Chapelyard; and who had struggled to this burying-ground, and literally entombed themselves in a small watch-house.... This shed is exactly seven feet long, by about six in breadth...on reaching this vault, I thrust my head through the hole of entrance, and had immediately to draw back, so intolerable was the effluvium; and, though rendered callous by a companionship for many years with disease and death, yet I was completely unnerved at the humble scene of suffering and misery that was presented to my view; six fellow creatures were almost buried alive in this filthy sepulcher. When they heard my voice, one called out, 'Is that the Priest?' another, 'Is that the Doctor?' The mother of the family begged in the most earnest manner that I would have them removed, or else that they would rot together; and they all implored that we would give them drink. Mr. Crowley produced the tea and sugar, but they said it was of no use to them, as they had no fire or place to light it in, and that what they wanted was water; that they had put a jug under the droppings from the roof, but would not have drink enough for the night. The next day I got the consent of the Poor Law Guardians to have my patients removed from this abode of the dead to the fever hospital, and they are since improving."

For those who were able to get help from the government, it may have seemed to many that moving into a house run by the government where all one's needs were met would be the answer to life's problems. However, this was far from true about the Poor Houses in 1840s Ireland. Families were torn apart, with fathers being housed in one section while mothers were sent to another and children to yet another. They were also terribly overcrowded and prone to outbreaks of disease. For instance, in December 1848, an epidemic of cholera wiped out huge portions of the population in workhouses across the country. Such plagues were common, and more often than not met, they were met by deaf ears among the government. In 1849, Lord Clarendon pleaded with his fellow ministers that "it is enough to drive one mad, day after day, to read the appeals that are made and meet them all with a negative...At Westport, and other places in Mayo, they have not a shilling to make preparations for the cholera, but no assistance can be given, and there is no credit for anything, as all our contractors are ruined. Surely this is a state of things to justify you asking the House of Commons for an advance, for I don't think there is another legislature in Europe that would disregard such suffering as now exists in the west of Ireland, or coldly persist in a policy of extermination." His request was not granted.

Clarendon

While 1847 was the worst year and would be forever known as Black '47, the famine hung on for several more years. For instance, in March 1849, one author observed, "A renewed and extensive failure of the potato crop has added greatly to the sufferings of the poor, and increased the perplexities which have involved all other classes of society. The burden of poor rates has become intolerable to a people who have been themselves the principal sufferers from the loss of their crops; and the prospect of the aggravation of the pressure during the ensuing year from the continued and increasing distress and destitution in the country, has paralyzed the energies of even the most sanguine and the most resolute. The peculiar evils of the present system of poor laws in Ireland, and their great inaptitude for such a country, has also naturally tended to check all exertion to prevent an increase of the rates, as the most active and well-disposed proprietor finds that all the employment he can give to his poor is of little avail without an extensive cooperation among his neighbors, which it is, from various causes, impracticable to attain, while the ill effects of a system by which such vast numbers are fed upon public doles have, it is too plain, only increased their indolence and indisposition to earn their bread by manly exertion. This system, continued in one shape or other since the Labor Rate Act was passed, while it is fast swallowing up all private property, has at the same time, produced incalculable evils, in rendering the mass of the population listless and dead to every feeling of independence, an effect peculiarly disastrous to the case of the Irish peasantry. Altogether the prospects of the country are most gloomy, the very opposite to those which a well-ordered state should exhibit."

This situation is not surprising, as even 21st century societies are constantly struggling to walk the fine line between aiding those in need and enabling those who have no need except for a little more ambition. 150 years ago, such problems were still new and exacerbated by the fact that the choice was often not between difficulty and comfort but between life and death. In May 1849, the *Cork Examiner* bemoaned the toll the famine was taking on the Irish economy while writing about Skibbereen Union, a community overwhelmed by the demands of the Poor Laws: "It is nearly 7000 pounds in debt to merchants for food; and while over 22,000 hungry paupers yearn for bread, which must be provided for them or they perish, there is not the least probability of a rate being collected from the farmers and occupiers who still remain in the country. We do most earnestly and in the name of humanity call on Government to take the case of Skibbereen, with its 22,000 paupers, and its bankrupt landlords, farmers and shopkeepers, into immediate consideration, and at once relieve the board from its embarrassment and this destitute from the near prospect of starvation and death. The Government must consider that beyond the credit of a single week's food once respectable house -- Messrs Gould and Co. -- have refused to grant, and that contractors are perfectly justified by the state of things in the neighboring town of Bantry, where all seems in hopeless ruin, in refusing to risk even a shilling's worth of their property on the faith of any board of guardians, be they paid or elected, the officers of the Government, or the representatives of the people."

Chapter 8: For the Relief of the Irish Nation

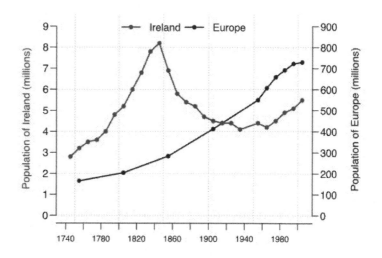

A graph indicating the population drop of Ireland and the contemporary population rise in the rest of Europe

"We arrived here on the 22nd from Liverpool. I regret to tell you that fever broke out, and that seventy passengers and one sailor were committed to the deep on the voyage. There are several more ill. We buried six yesterday on shore. The carpenter and joiner are occupied making coffins. There are six more dead after the night. I cannot say when we can go to Quebec, as we cannot land the remainder of the sick at present, there being no room in the hospitals for them, though the front of the island is literally covered with sheds and tents. The accounts from the shore are awful, and our condition on board you can form no idea of— helpless children without parents or relatives, the father buried in the deep last week, and the mother the week before— their six children under similar unfortunate circumstances, and so on. I trust God will carry me through this trying ordeal— I was a few days sick, but am now recovered. Captain Wilson was complaining for a few days. It is an awful change from the joyous hopes with which most of us left our unfortunate country, expecting to be able to earn that livelihood denied us at home— all— all changed in many cases to bitter deep despair." - Letter from an anonymous Irish immigrant to Canada

In one sense, evicting families did solve the problem of long-term success for many Irish men and women who, when faced with the prospect of losing their homes, made the gut-wrenching decision to emigrate to either England or North America. John Whyte was one of those who made that decision and confided in his journal on May 30, 1847, "Many and deep are the wounds that the sensitive heart inflicts upon its possessor, as he journeys through life's pilgrimage but on few occasions are they so acutely felt as when one is about to part from those who formed a portion of his existence; deeper still pierces the pang as the idea presents itself that the separation may be forever, but when one feels a father's nervous grasp, a dear sister's tender, sobbing embrace and the eye wanders around the apartment, drinking in each familiar object, until it rests upon the vacant chair which she who nursed his helpless infancy was wont to occupy, then the agony he wishes to conceal becomes insupportable. But as the skilful surgeon tears off the bandage which the hand of affection gently withdraws from the wound, thereby unconsciously inflicting greater pain, so it is better not to linger upon the affecting scene but rush suddenly away."

In the decade between 1845 and 1855, almost 3 million men, women and children left Ireland forever, bound for new homes in North America, Australia or other parts of Great Britain. The most fortunate were sent to these far off lands by their former landlords, who found it a better financial deal than continuing to rent small plots of land out. In fact, the years of the Irish Potato Famine saw many landlords shift from having many small-scale tenants renting their property to consolidating their land into large tracts that could support sheep or dairy farming.

Through the years, this has led some to suspect that the English government deliberately caused the blight that led to the famine, and while this is unlikely, it is true that many a calloused politician observed that it ultimately solved the problem of overpopulation in Ireland. Charles Edward Trevelyan, the British Treasury Secretary for Ireland, wrote as far back as 1846 that with overpopulation "being altogether beyond the power of man, the cure has been applied by the direct stroke of an all-wise Providence in a manner as unexpected and as unthought of as it is likely to be effectual." In 1848, with an estimated million or more Irish already dead, he commented, "The matter is awfully serious, but we are in the hands of Providence, without a possibility of averting the catastrophe if it is to happen. We can only wait the result." Some months later, he asserted, "The great evil with which we have to contend is not the physical evil of the famine, but the moral evil of the selfish, perverse and turbulent character of the people." Likewise, in 1848, the English Chancellor of the Exchequer, wrote to a friend who owned an estate in Ireland: "I am not at all appalled by your tenantry going. That seems to be a necessary part of the process...We must not complain of what we really want to obtain."

Still, there were those who cared and were concerned about the direction the country was taking. When Edward Twisleton, then serving as a Poor Law Commissioner, resigned because he could not get enough help from Britain to save those he was to serve, the Earl of Clarendon told the Prime Minister, Lord Russell, "He thinks that the destitution here [in Ireland] is so horrible, and the indifference of the House of Commons is so manifest, that he is an unfit agent for a policy that must be one of extermination."

Tragically, many Irishmen who left Ireland learned that they were no better off once they were on board the ships than they had been at home. Many unscrupulous men, attracted by the easy money to be had carrying large numbers of poor people to new homes, turned ships formerly used for shipping grain or cattle into passenger vessels. In doing so, however, they only made the most minimum changes possible, and many who boarded the ships, already weakened from years of starvation, did not live long enough to see their new homes. In fact, the ships were so notoriously bad that they earned the nickname "coffin ships." In August 1847, *The Toronto Globe* in Canada reported, "The *Virginius* from Liverpool, with 496 passengers, had lost 158 by death, nearly one third of the whole, and she had 180 sick; above one half of the whole will never see their home in the New World. A medical officer at the quarantine station on Grosse lie off Quebec reported that 'the few who were able to come on deck were ghastly, yellow-looking specters, unshaven and hollow-cheeked. . . not more than six or eight were really healthy and able to exert themselves. The crew of the ship were all ill, and seven had died. On the *Erin's Queen* 78 passengers had died and 104 were sick. On this ship the captain had to bribe the seamen with a sovereign for each body brought out from the hold. The dead sometimes had to be dragged out with boat hooks, since even their own relatives refused to touch them."

During the years of the Great Famine, emigration from Ireland reached a record 250,000 in one year. Whyte was typical of those leaving, in that he was young and unattached, while those who were married or had family commitments tended to stay and tried to survive where they were. According to a report released in 1851, "The emigration of the last three years gives an annual average of 268,469 persons, being not very short of the whole annual increase of the United Kingdom. If this emigration be analysed, the results as regards Ireland will be much more striking. For assuming nine-tenths of the emigration from Liverpool to be Irish (which is a low estimate), and even omitting altogether those who proceed from the Clyde, it will appear that the Irish emigration during the last three years has been 601,448; giving an average of 200,482 a year. Now the increase of population in Ireland between 1831 and 1841 as appears from the census return, was 407,723, in spite of an emigration amounting during the same years to 455,239, thus making the real increase to be 802,959, or 86,295 a year. Assuming the increase to have been at the same rate since 1841, when the population was returned at 8,175,238, it would give for the eight years to the close of 1849, 707,480 souls, or 88,435 per annum. At this rate, therefore, the population would be decreased in about in about eight years in about eight years by 1,000,000 souls by emigration alone; when it is also taken into account that the emigration comprises a large proportion of those who are in the vigour of life, and on whom the increase of our population chiefly depends, it may be assumed that its influence in checking such increase is even greater than the mere figures imply."

For those who survived, few though they were, the end of the famine in 1851 marked a time of new beginning, a time when land was actually more available, not less, and when workers were needed and could expect at least decent wages. The misery and resentment that the Irish had towards the British also led to further calls for independence. A German philosopher once wrote,

"That which doesn't kill me makes me stronger." For the people who survived the Irish Potato Famine, truer words were never spoken.

A memorial to victims

A mural in Belfast about the Famine

A memorial in Dublin

Bibliography

Donnelly, James S (2005), *The Great Irish Potato Famine*, Sutton Publishing.

Gray, Peter (1995), *The Irish Famine*, New York: Harry N. Abrams, Inc.

Hayden, Tom (1998), Hayden, Tom; O'Connor, Garrett; Harty, Patricia, eds., *Irish hunger: personal reflections on the legacy of the famine*, Roberts Rinehart Publishers.

Laxton, Edward (1997), *The Famine Ships: The Irish Exodus to America 1846–51*, Bloomsbury.

Litton, Helen (1994), *The Irish Famine: An Illustrated History*, Wolfhound Press.

Ó Gráda, Cormac (1993), *Ireland before and after the Famine: Explorations in Economic History 1800–1925*, Manchester University Press.

Ó Gráda, Cormac (2000), *Black '47 and Beyond: The Great Irish Famine in History, Economy, and Memory*, Princeton University Press.

Ó Gráda, Cormac (2006), *Ireland's Great Famine: Interdisciplinary Perspectives*, Dublin Press.

Póirtéir, Cathal (1995), *The Great Irish Famine*, RTÉ/Mercier Press.

Made in the USA
Las Vegas, NV
06 November 2023